Blindness

Designed and produced by
Aladdin Books Ltd
70 Old Compton Street
London W1V 5PA

First published in the
United States in 1989 by
Franklin Watts
387 Park Avenue South
New York NY 10016

Design: David West Children's Book Design
Editor: Zuza Vrbova
Picture Research: Cecilia Weston-Baker
Illustrator: Stuart Brendon

Printed in Belgium

Library of Congress Cataloging-in-Publication Data

Parker, Steve.
    Living with blindness.
    Includes index.
    Summary: Explains how the eye works and examines the
causes the blindness and other eye disorders. Also
discusses eye care and how to cope with impaired eyesight.
ISBN 0-531-10843-0
    1. Blindness. [1. Blind] I. Title. II. Title:
Blindness.
RE91.P32 1989
617.7'12   89-9091
                                         CIP
                                         AC

CONTENTS

Living with

Blindness

Steve Parker

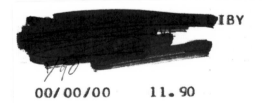
FRANKLIN WATTS
New York : London : Toronto : Sydney

HOW THE EYE WORKS

Our eyes are one of our most precious senses, our "windows on the world." It is estimated that through them comes four-fifths of everything we know. We use them to recognize the face of a friend, to read facts in a book, enjoy the colors of flowers, play with a computer game, and lots more, every day. Each eye has an outer wall that is made of several layers. The sclera on the outside is tough and whitish, and forms a strong outer skin. Inside this is the deep red choroid, a layer rich in blood vessels that nourish the other parts of the eye. Within the choroid at the back of the eye is the retina, the layer that picks up light rays coming in through the lens at the front of the eye. The pattern of light is turned into nerve signals which pass along the optic nerve to the brain. The vitreous humor gives the eye its firm, spherical shape.

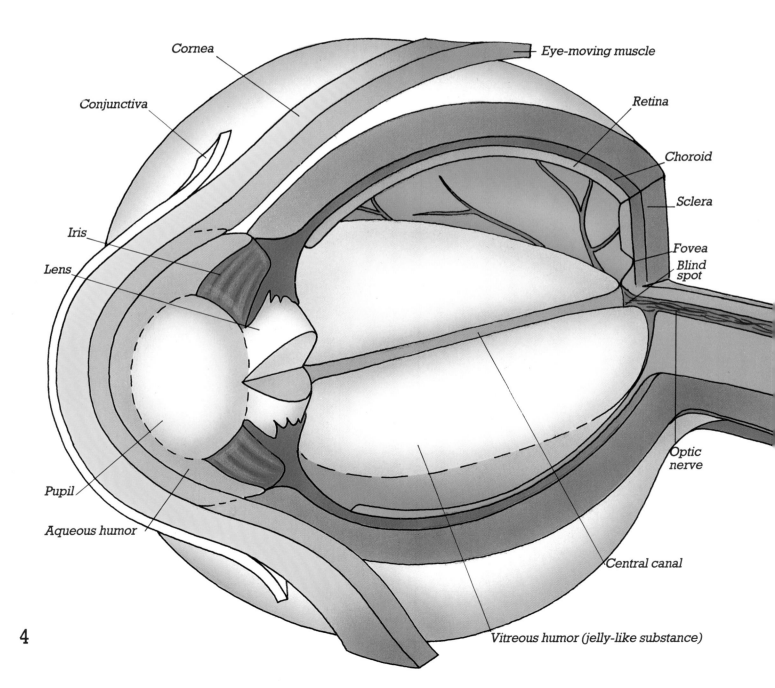

Cornea

Conjunctiva

Eye-moving muscle

Retina

Choroid

Sclera

Iris

Fovea

Blind spot

Lens

Pupil

Aqueous humor

Optic nerve

Central canal

Vitreous humor (jelly-like substance)

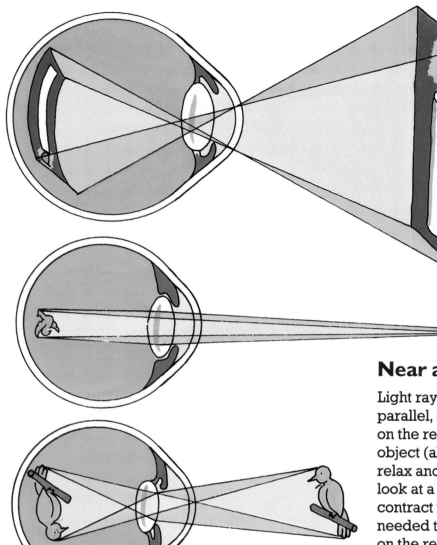

Forming an image

Light rays pass through the conjunctiva and cornea, then travel through the aqueous humor, through a hole in the iris (the pupil) and on through the lens and vitreous humor to the retina. The curved shapes of the cornea and lens "bend" the rays into focus on the retina, to form an image.

Near and faraway objects

Light rays from a distant object are almost parallel, and need little bending to focus them on the retina. So when you look at a faraway object (above) the muscles around the lens relax and the lens changes shape. When you look at a close object (left) the muscles contract to make the lens into the shape needed to bend the rays more and form them on the retina.

Controlling light

Muscles in the iris can shorten or relax, to make the pupil bigger or smaller. In bright light, the pupil closes almost to a pinpoint (below left). In dim light, the pupil enlarges to let in as much light as possible (below right).

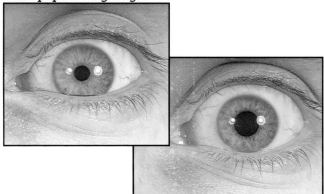

Small pupil in bright light

Large pupil in dim light

An inverted world?

The lens in the eye forms an inverted image on the retina. The brain adjusts this so that we see things the right way up. You can demonstrate this by casting an image through a magnifying glass. The magnifying glass acts as a lens and the image formed is upside down.

5

Seeing in color

In the retina, there are two kinds of light-sensitive cells, called rods and cones. There are more than 120 million rods and 7 million cones in each eye. The rods are very sensitive and detect low levels of light, and are concerned with black and white vision. So they "see" in dim conditions, but only in black and white (or rather, shades of gray). The cones work well only in bright light, but they can detect colors. There are three main types of cones, each responding to light of certain colors: reds, greens, or blues. The brain compares which kinds of cones are stimulated the most in each tiny area of retina, and so works out the color of the image in that area. Cones are concentrated in a minute pit-shaped area at the back of the retina known as the yellow spot, or fovea. The part of the image focused there is seen most clearly and in greatest detail. Rods are more numerous around the sides and edges of the retina, toward the front of the eye.

Seeing at night

Cones do not work well in dim light, so we see colors less clearly in these conditions and the yellow spot becomes an almost "blank" area. We therefore have to rely more on rods. Looking slightly to one side of an object, so that its image falls on the rods, which are more plentiful at the edges of the retina, often gives a clearer view.

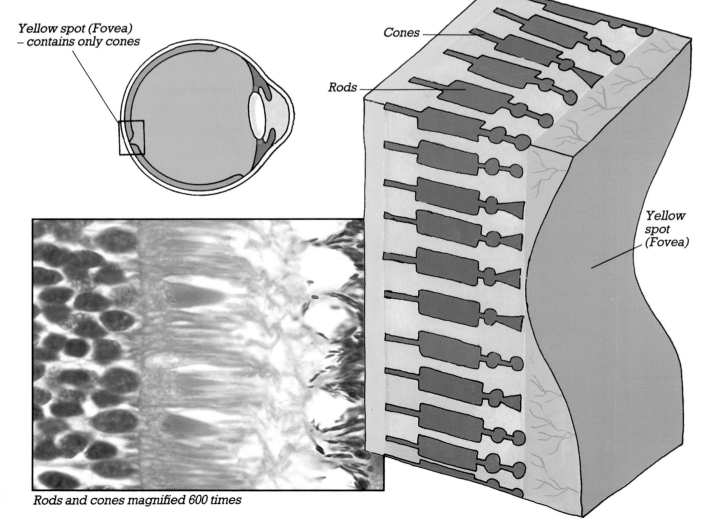

Yellow spot (Fovea)
– contains only cones

Cones

Rods

Yellow spot (Fovea)

Rods and cones magnified 600 times

"Seeing" in the brain

We see *with* our eyes, but not *in* our eyes. The eye is a sophisticated sensor. It detects patterns of light rays, generates electrical nerve signals from them, processes and simplifies these signals, and sends the results to the brain. The signals pass through a series of nerve pathways inside the brain, such as the optic chiasma, where they are further sorted. Finally, most of the nerve signals reach an area located low down in the brain, known as the visual cortex. In this region, the signals are decoded, interpreted and compared with memories. The visual cortex perceives light and shade and the position of objects. This is how and where we make our "mental picture" of the world.

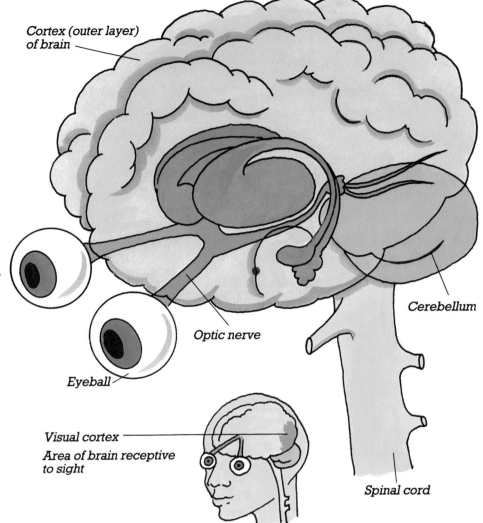

Cortex (outer layer) of brain

Cerebellum

Optic nerve

Eyeball

Visual cortex
Area of brain receptive to sight

Spinal cord

Why do we have two eyes?

Our two eyes see similar views of the world. But the views are different enough for the brain to compare them and judge the distance of an object (known as stereoscopic vision). You can perform a simple experiment to show that this is true. With both eyes open, use a pencil at arm's length to touch a spot on a piece of paper. This is not too difficult. Close one eye and try again. It is harder because you cannot judge distance so well with only one eye. People who have lost their sight in one eye only, through an accident or an illness, can see but find it hard to do certain things – pouring a drink from a pitcher into a glass, for example.

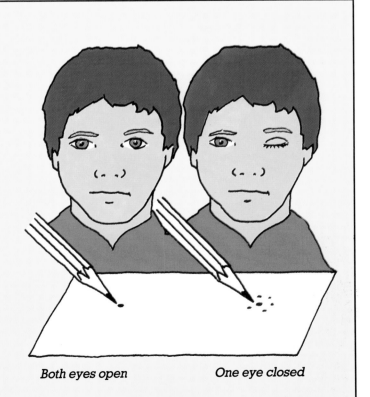

Both eyes open   One eye closed

7

VISUAL PROBLEMS

Body parts grow to different sizes in different people. Big hands or little feet may not be a problem. But for eyes, a small change in size can be important. In some people, the eyes are too large or small in relation to the power of the cornea and lens to focus light rays. The result is a visual defect such as far or nearsighted, in which an area of vision is blurred. This is not a disease, but a result of the way the body develops. The eyes are also delicate and exposed. They cannot be covered by tough skin, because light has to pass into them. Eyelids close quickly if something comes too near, and blink regularly to smear a moistening film of tears across the front of the eye, washing away dust. However this damp surface is attractive to germs, which can infect the front of the eye and also cause sight problems. One common kind of problem, which can lead to blindness, is associated with the rods and cones. If they cease to function or die, it can lead to retinitis pigmentosa.

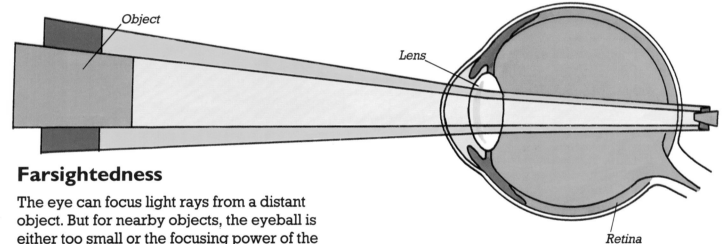

Farsightedness

The eye can focus light rays from a distant object. But for nearby objects, the eyeball is either too small or the focusing power of the lens is too weak. Rays cannot be bent enough to bring them into focus on reaching the retina.

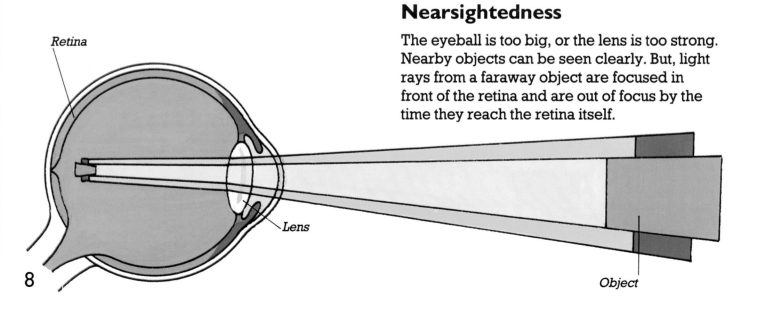

Nearsightedness

The eyeball is too big, or the lens is too strong. Nearby objects can be seen clearly. But, light rays from a faraway object are focused in front of the retina and are out of focus by the time they reach the retina itself.

Out of focus – far and nearsightedness

Seeing roses with farsightedness

Seeing roses with nearsightedness

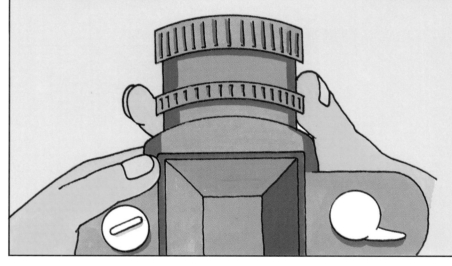

Farsightedness and nearsightedness give different views of the same scene, in a similar way to a camera that has been set to the wrong focus. In the past, this could have caused problems for people. But nowadays eyeglasses or contact lenses can easily correct the problem.

Eye tests

Visual defects such as nearsightedness or farsightedness often develop gradually. Some people do not notice that their eyesight is not as good as it used to be. This is one reason for having a regular sight test and eye examination every one to two years. Another reason is to check for early signs of any eye damage or disease, so that it can be treated without delay.

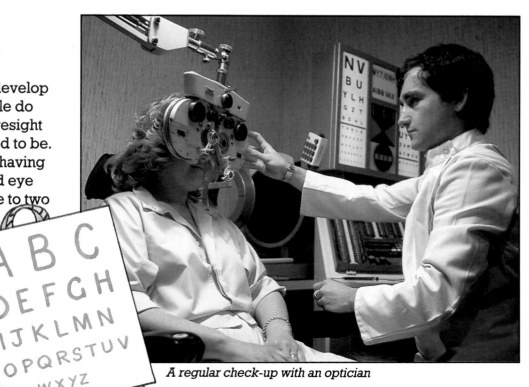

A regular check-up with an optician

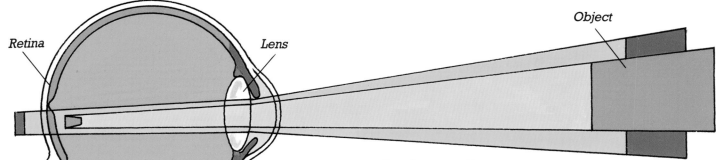

Astigmatism

In a normal eye, the curvatures of the cornea and lens conform to focus the image onto the retina. In astigmatism, the curvatures of the cornea, lens and retina do not match and so only parts of the image are in focus, the rest is blurred.

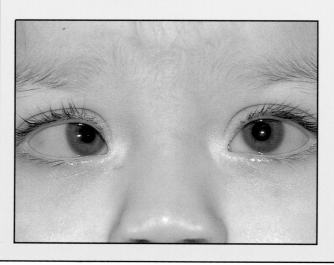

The six main muscles that move the eyeball

Squint

Normally, both eyes swivel to look directly at the same object. In a squint (also called cross-eye) the two eyes do not look at the same thing. This may be due to a problem in one or more of the six muscles that move each eyeball, or in the nerves controlling them. A muscle may be weak and not turn the eye enough, or it may be over-tight and pull the eye around too much. The problem can be corrected by wearing an eye-patch or by surgery.

"Color blindness"

To some people, "color blindness" means looking out at a world in just black, white and shades of gray. But complete color deficiency in this form is very rare, affecting only 1 person in about 40,000. Various forms of partial color deficiency are more common, in which most colors can be picked out clearly, but a few are hard to identify accurately or to tell apart. These problems are usually caused by the poor function or lack of one type of cone cell and can be inherited. For example, in red-green color blindness (anomalopia) it is difficult to see the difference between certain shades of red and green. Because of the way it is inherited, this problem affects about 1 in 12 men but only 1 in 200 women.

Normal vision

Red-green color deficiency

Blue-yellow color deficiency

Complete color deficiency (monochromatic vision)

"Night blindness"

If there is a lack of vitamin A (retinol) in the body – which is in foods like fish, carrots and other fresh vegetables and dairy products – the rod cells cannot make enough of their light-sensitive substance called rhodopsin. This means they do not work well in dim light, leading to the condition called "night blindness."

Normal rod　　　　*Retinol-deficient rod*

11

Conjunctivitis

The conjunctiva, the thin and delicate layer at the front of the eye, sometimes becomes red, swollen and sore. This inflammation is called conjunctivitis. It may be caused by an allergy such as hay fever, or by germs that infect the surface of the eye. The eyes become itchy and painful, and there may be a discharge of watery fluid or thicker, yellowish pus. In some cases, sight becomes temporarily misty. Various drugs such as antibiotics or anti-inflammatories, usually given as eyedrops, help to cure the problem. A newborn baby's eyes can be infected from the mother during birth with the germs that cause the sexually transmitted disease, gonorrhoea. This can be serious if it is left untreated.

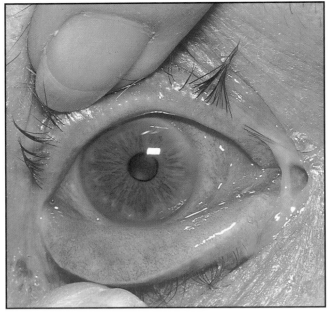

Inflammation of the membranes around the eye

Trachoma

This is a severe form of conjunctivitis. The coverings of the eyes become infected with a bacterial germ called *Chlamydia trachomatis*. If it is not treated with antibiotic drugs, the eyes become inflamed, sore and eventually scarred. Trachoma is most common in hot, dry areas and can be carried by flies. It affects an estimated 400 million people. Many millions have been partly or completely blinded by this infection. It is one of the leading causes of blindness in the world.

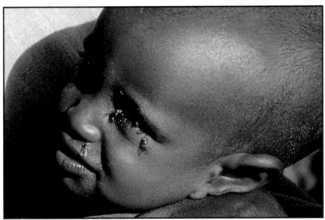

In Africa and Asia flies can spread trachoma

"Seeing stars"

"Scintillating scotoma" form of migraine aura

The brain sometimes "sees" things that are not really there. A knock on the back of the head, near the visual cortex, can make you "see stars." This is because the brain has been jolted and disturbed.

In the severe kind of headache called migraine, a sufferer may experience an "aura," such as a shimmering or zig-zag pattern around objects, before the main headache begins. A migraine is sometimes caused by tension, which affects the muscles around the eyeball. This is why the sufferer sometimes feels as though the eye is being pulled into the head.

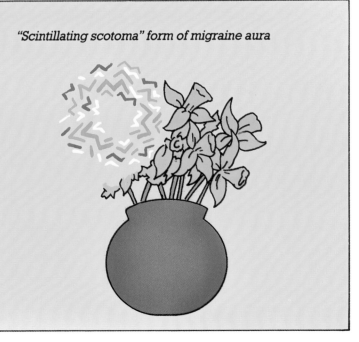

Drugs and alcohol

Any drug that affects muscle coordination or the workings of the brain can affect eyesight. After several alcoholic drinks, the brain cannot accurately control the muscles that move the eyeballs. Instead of pointing at the same object, the eyes "wander." Also the brain becomes less able to combine the two images from the two eyes. The result is blurring of sight and "double vision," which causes someone to see two scenes side by side. Alcohol does affect people in different ways. Some people feel very dizzy, as though they have been on a roundabout. Besides these physical effects, alcohol can change how people feel and understand the world. Some types of medical drugs, such as those used to treat depression or epilepsy, can also cause blurred vision.

"Tunnel vision"

Somebody with "tunnel vision" can see only a small area of the normal visual field in front of them. It is as though they were looking through a tube or along a tunnel. There are various causes, including some glaucomas and eye tumors. Rarely is a person born with the condition, and can see only one-twentieth of the normal visual field.

Interpreting images

Our brain makes constant readjustments and alterations to the mass of images that we perceive from the outside world. If an electronic picture was made of the nerce impulses falling on the retina, without the help of the brain's subtle interpretation of meaning, the resulting visual picture would simply comprise a series of uneven and confusing spots of light. The brain constantly adjusts the familiar colors and shapes of the outside world, always trying to find a sensible meaning to anything we see.

Hallucinations

The way the brain interprets what the eyes detect is extremely complicated. A drug that affects the brain's chemistry and the way nerve signals are handled can interfere with vision, so that the person experiences hallucinations and "sees false images." Although hallucinations seem to come from the eyes, they are images made up in the brain itself. Various drugs such as marijuana, mescaline and LSD produce this effect and are known as hallucinogens. Other causes are extreme tiredness, a high fever and mental illness.

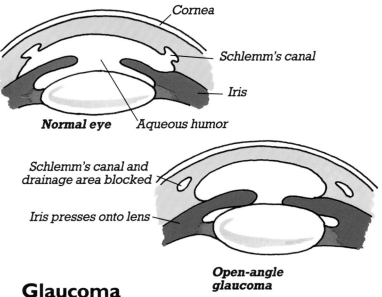

Normal eye

- Cornea
- Schlemm's canal
- Iris
- Aqueous humor

- Schlemm's canal and drainage area blocked
- Iris presses onto lens

Open-angle glaucoma

EXAMINING THE EYE

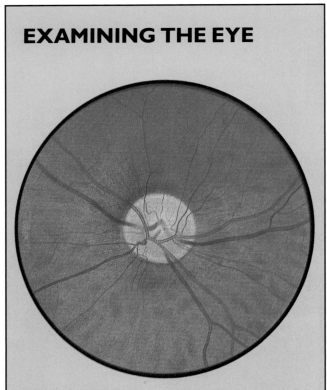

A doctor or optician looks into the eye using an ophthalmoscope. A light beam is shone through the pupil onto the retina (above) and a lens system in the ophthalmoscope focuses the view. The eye's own lens also acts as a magnifier. This test is a good check for all kinds of eye problems. It reveals signs of general conditions such as high blood pressure or diabetes.

Glaucoma

The aqueous humor, the fluid in front of the lens, is constantly being made by the ciliary part of the eye. Normally it drains away between the iris and cornea into a tiny tube, Schlemm's canal, and then into small veins outside the eye. In the various types of glaucoma, the fluid cannot drain away properly. Pressure builds up in the eye, and may damage the delicate nerves and blood vessels of the retina. This can cause blurred or hazy sight, loss of visual field, and pain and redness in the eye and eventually blindness.

Detached retina

In rare cases the light-sensitive retina, inside the eye, comes away from the choroid layer next to it. Either the entire thickness of the retina lifts away, or the retina itself splits into two layers and the inner one detaches. Usually the process is gradual, and begins over a small area toward the front of the retina, near the lens. Fluid from the choroid seeps into the space, or vitreous humor may pass through a tear in the retina to fill the space. Signs include flashes of light, "curtains" or "cobwebs" of distorted vision, and cloudy or dim sight (especially around the edges of the visual field). If it is not treated, dark areas may form where sight is lost. This condition is more likely to affect people who are nearsighted or have had an eye injury.

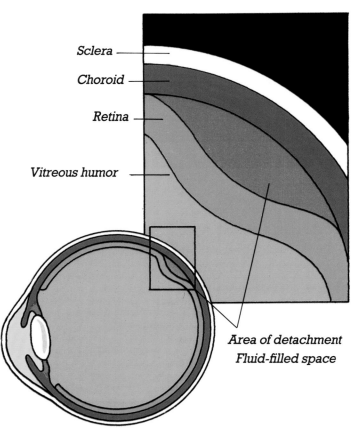

- Sclera
- Choroid
- Retina
- Vitreous humor

Area of detachment
Fluid-filled space

Cataract

A cataract is a cloudiness or mistiness in the lens of the eye. The clouding of a cataract tends to appear in old age, or after an injury or inflammation. It may also be linked with diabetes. A cataract is not a growth, like a tumor, but a change in the nature of the lens substance itself. It's a bit like an egg white turning solid and opaque after being cooked. The clear jelly-like material in the lens turns cloudy. This causes the distorted or misty sight. In the early stages the visual problems are hardly noticeable. Later, the cataract may be visible through the pupil as a whitish area inside the lens. It can lead to loss of vision.

Children who are born blind sometimes have a congenital cataract. This means that the clouding of the lens is present when the child is born. A cataract cannot be remedied and does not deteriorate by uncaring habits such as reading in low lighting levels. The most successful way of treating cataracts is removing the lens (see page 18) under a local or general anesthetic. Healing and permanent adjustment takes three months. After the operation, the lack of a lens to focus light entering the eye is overcome by using eyeglasses or contact lenses, or by inserting an artificial lens.

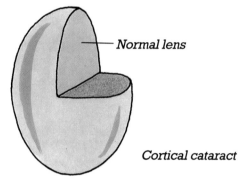

Normal lens

Cortical cataract

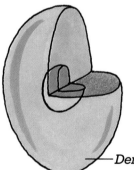

A cataract may appear in the central part of the lens, called the nucleus. Or it may develop in the outer area, known as the cortex, which is formed after birth.

Dense nuclear cataract

Problems in the brain

A brain disorder can cause sight problems. If a person has a stroke, part of one side of the brain is "starved" of blood, because of a blocked or burst blood vessel. Alternatively, blood may leak from a vessel and press on the brain tissue, damaging it (subdural hemorrhage). Control of the eye-moving muscles may go astray, causing double vision. In a severe case, sight in one eye can be lost.

Normal vision   *After stroke – vision lost in one eye*

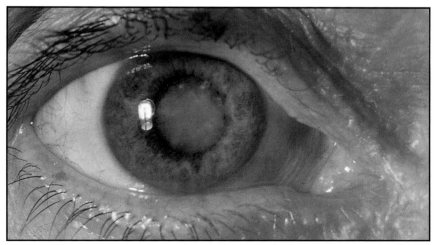

The eye of an elderly person with a cataract

TREATMENT OF EYE DISORDERS

We rely on our eyes for so many everyday tasks, from crossing a road to pouring a drink into a cup. We learn with our eyes, by reading books, watching television and studying diagrams and photographs. We also enjoy with our eyes – looking at works of art or making models and crafts. So anything that interferes with eyesight can cause drastic problems. Visual defects such as near or farsightedness are usually easily dealt with, by eyeglasses or contact lenses. Modern medical drugs treat conditions such as glaucoma and eye infections, with the minimum of side-effects. New surgical techniques can reach inside the eye to reattach a detached retina or break up a cataract. As with any health problem, the sooner an eye disorder is detected and action taken, then the more likely it is to be treated successfully or cured. Although many people do have eye disorders, most of the problems can be cured. Only ten percent of registered blind people are totally without sight.

Concave lens

View with corrective lens

View without corrective lens

Correcting nearsightedness

The lens for correcting nearsightedness has a concave (inward-curved) shape. This bends the light rays outward, so that the misshapen lens in the eye can focus an image onto the retina, rather than in front of it.

16

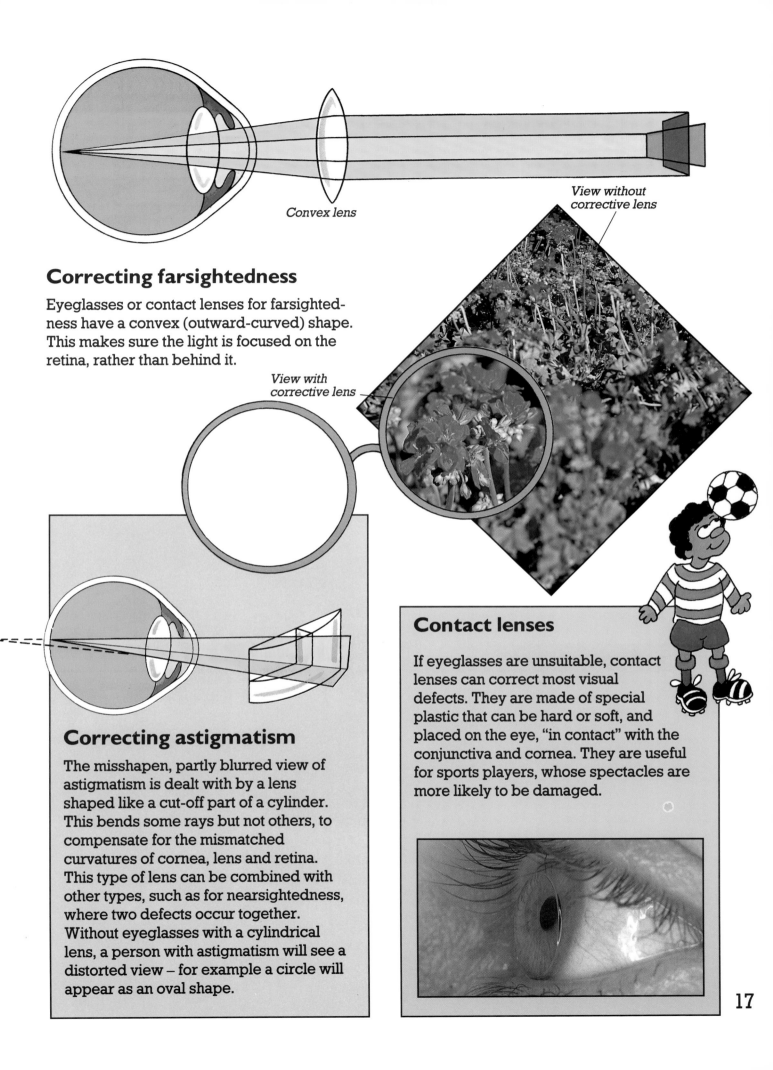

Convex lens

View without corrective lens

Correcting farsightedness

Eyeglasses or contact lenses for farsighted-ness have a convex (outward-curved) shape. This makes sure the light is focused on the retina, rather than behind it.

View with corrective lens

Correcting astigmatism

The misshapen, partly blurred view of astigmatism is dealt with by a lens shaped like a cut-off part of a cylinder. This bends some rays but not others, to compensate for the mismatched curvatures of cornea, lens and retina. This type of lens can be combined with other types, such as for nearsightedness, where two defects occur together. Without eyeglasses with a cylindrical lens, a person with astigmatism will see a distorted view – for example a circle will appear as an oval shape.

Contact lenses

If eyeglasses are unsuitable, contact lenses can correct most visual defects. They are made of special plastic that can be hard or soft, and placed on the eye, "in contact" with the conjunctiva and cornea. They are useful for sports players, whose spectacles are more likely to be damaged.

Cataract removal

There are several modern methods for removing cataracts, which have saved the sight of millions of people around the world. One technique is emulsification-aspiration. The surgeon makes a cut, only one tenth-of-an inch wide, in the side of the eye, at the junction of the transparent cornea and whitish sclera, using a diamond-tipped knife. A small probe is then inserted through and into the lens. The probes ultrasonic tip vibrates up to 40,000 times each second and causes the cloudy lens substance to break into tiny fragments (emulsify). The fragments are sucked out (aspirated) by another device in the probe's tip. The rear part of the lens capsule (the tough "bag" around the lens) may be left intact, to keep the aqueous humor, in the front of the eye, separate from the vitreous humor.

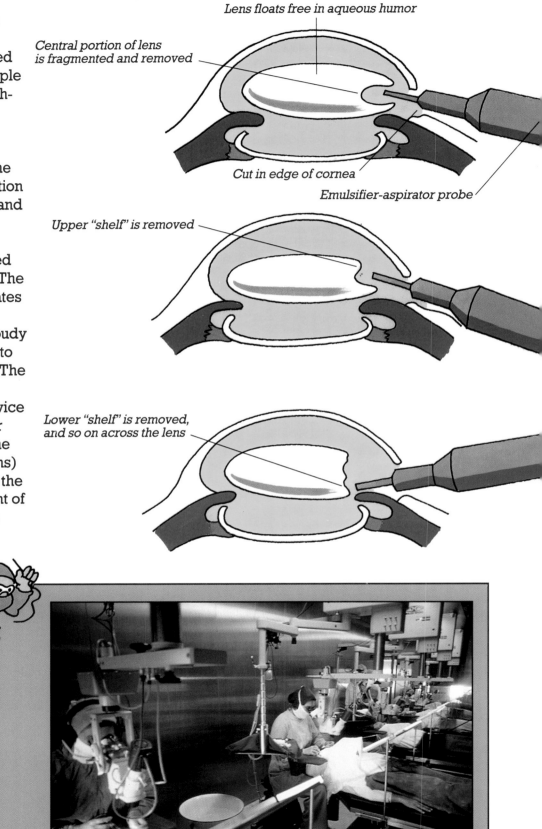

Lens floats free in aqueous humor

Central portion of lens is fragmented and removed

Cut in edge of cornea

Emulsifier-aspirator probe

Upper "shelf" is removed

Lower "shelf" is removed, and so on across the lens

A "production line" of eye operations in the Soviet Union

Mass sight saving

In some countries, such as the Soviet Union and China, cataract removal operations are carried out on a "production line." Up-to-date equipment involves the tiniest of incisions in the eye, and especially fine stitches to close the incision afterward. This lessens the risk of infection or other complications.

Artificial lenses

Removing a cataract-clouded lens can save a person from becoming blind. But it makes the eye extremely farsighted and unable to focus sharply. This can be helped to a great degree by special cataract eyeglasses or contact lenses. Alternatively, an artificial plastic lens can be implanted into the eye, in place of the natural one. The new lens is often implanted just after the diseased one is removed, during the same operation and through the same incision. There are various designs of artificial lenses. Most have a central lens part made of a clear plastic, known as PMMA, with struts, flanges or nylon loops to hold it in place inside the eye. The artificial lens may be positioned in front of the iris (anterior chamber) within the pupil, and held in place by the iris itself (iris-supported), or behind the iris (posterior chamber) where the original lens was. After a few weeks, fibrous scar tissue grows around the edge of the lens and helps to hold it firmly in place.

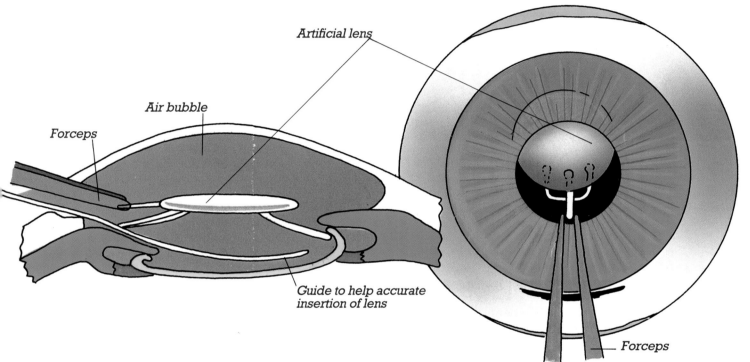

Forceps

Air bubble

Artificial lens

Guide to help accurate insertion of lens

Forceps

New lens for old

Implanting an artificial lens is a delicate operation. The eye's front chamber is drained of fluid and an air bubble inserted. This holds the cornea away from the new lens. Otherwise, the plastic would stick to the inner layer of cornea and tear it. The lens is slid carefully into position along a plastic guide, using fine forceps. The front chamber is refilled with body fluid and the cut is sealed. All items must be totally sterile, to keep germs out of the eye.

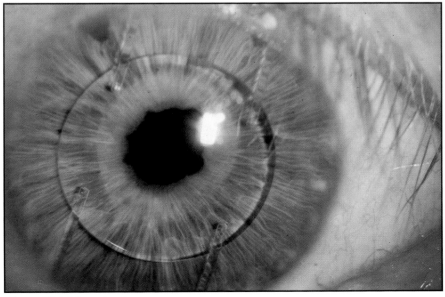

An artificial lens in place

19

"Lazy" eyes

In a squint, the brain is confused by the differing images it receives. It tends to ignore one image and concentrate on the other. After a time the ignored eye and the part of the brain dealing with its image become "lazy," and see in less and less detail. To prevent this, a patch is worn over the good eye for several hours each day, so the "lazy" eye is used again. The boy in the picture is five years old and used to wearing a patch for a time every day.

Correcting a squint

Eye movements rely on the close coordination of the six muscles that control each eyeball. Some types of squint can be helped by surgery to adjust the muscles. If carried out early in the development of a squint, this stops the squinting eye from becoming "lazy" and losing the ability to see. It is also helpful for psychological reasons. The appearance of a severe squint is unsettling to some people, and this can affect the confidence of the person with the squint. In the operation, the surgeon pulls the eyeball forward slightly to reach the muscles behind. A fold ("tuck") can be put in one or more muscles, or a short piece of muscle may be removed and the ends rejoined. This pulls the eyeball around slightly to remedy the squint.

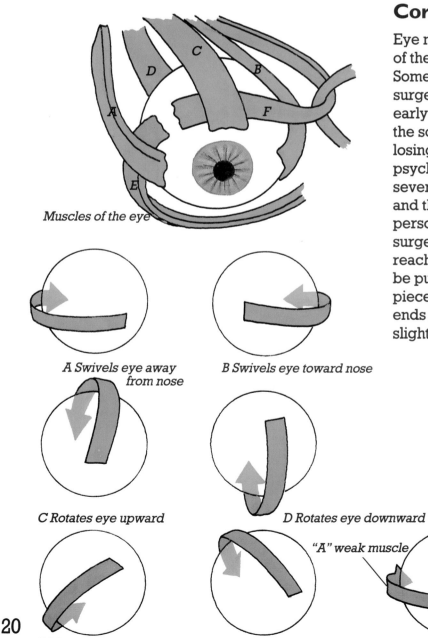

Muscles of the eye

A Swivels eye away from nose

B Swivels eye toward nose

C Rotates eye upward

D Rotates eye downward

E Moves eye down and outward

F Moves eye up and outward

"A" weak muscle

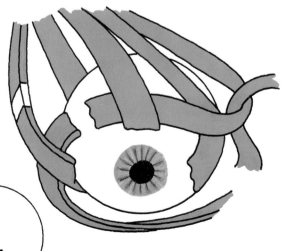

Section removed from weak lateral rectus muscle that swivels the eye away from the nose (A) so the eye is pulled round to the right.

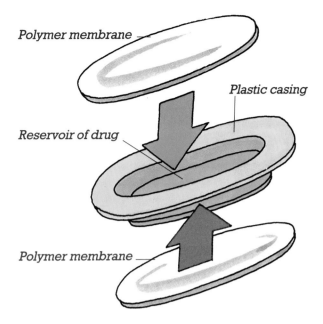

Polymer membrane

Plastic casing

Reservoir of drug

Polymer membrane

Drug implants

Several eye disorders, such as glaucoma, can be treated with modern drugs. These are usually given as eyedrops. But drops can be awkward to put in, especially for elderly people, and a dose is sometimes forgotten or too many drops are given by mistake. A newer method is to enclose a "gel reservoir" containing the drug in a special plastic case, with polymer membrane sides. This is carefully positioned under the eyelid. The gel slowly dissolves and releases the drug at a regular rate through the membrane.

Surgery for glaucoma

Operations to cure glaucoma are nowadays very successful and most take less than an hour. In a common version, called iridectomy, a cut is made at the junction of the cornea and sclera. Through this a small strip of iris is cut away. This makes a path for the aqueous humor to drain from the front chamber of the eye, so lowering the pressure inside the eyeball. In another version, the glaucoma drainage operation, a channel is cut for the aqueous humor to flow from the eye.

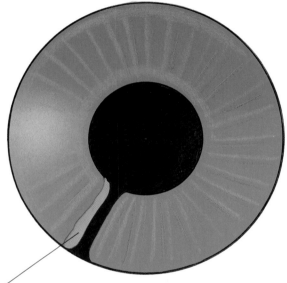

Cut in iris relieves internal pressure

Corneal transplant

Scarring or mistiness of the cornea, from repeated eye infections or corneal ulcers, can eventually cause partial blindness. In a corneal transplant, a cornea taken from the donor's body is grafted in place of the scarred one. The new cornea usually "takes" well, as this part of the eye has no blood supply and so the new cornea cannot be attacked and rejected by the body's immune defense system.

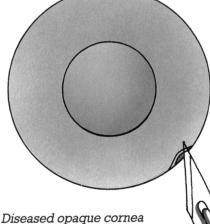

Diseased opaque cornea cut away

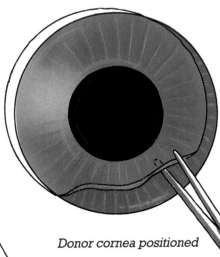

Donor cornea positioned

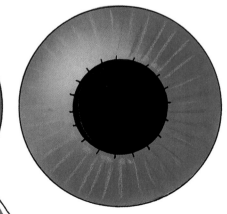

Donor cornea secured with fine stitches

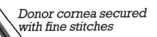

Laser surgery

The invention of the intense light beam known as the laser has given surgeons a powerful new tool – the "laser scalpel." The laser beam can be controlled and focused precisely to cut, destroy or "weld" body tissues, by a process known as "laser photocoagulation." As the beam cuts, it seals tiny blood vessels, so that the incision does not bleed too much. The laser scalpel is particularly useful for the eye specialist (ophthalmologist or ophthalmic surgeon). Using a special frame, the patient's head is held steady. A small contact lens with three "mirrors" may be placed over the eye to aid focusing on a particular part of the retina.

The surgeon views the inside of the eye through a magnifying system, and the laser beam can be "fired" along this line of sight. Many hundreds of tiny "burns" may be needed to treat some conditions. Each time the patient sees a flash of light, but the procedure is painless, and usually only a sedative or local anesthetic is needed. The beam can be used to seal leaking blood vessels, as sometimes happens in the condition known as diabetic retinopathy. This affects some people who have diabetes. The tiny blood vessels in the retina become fragile and break, and blood leaks under the retina or into the vitreous humor, making it cloudy. The laser can also treat detached retina, and some cases of macular degeneration, in which the blood supply to the macula (the region at the back of the retina, around the yellow spot) fails.

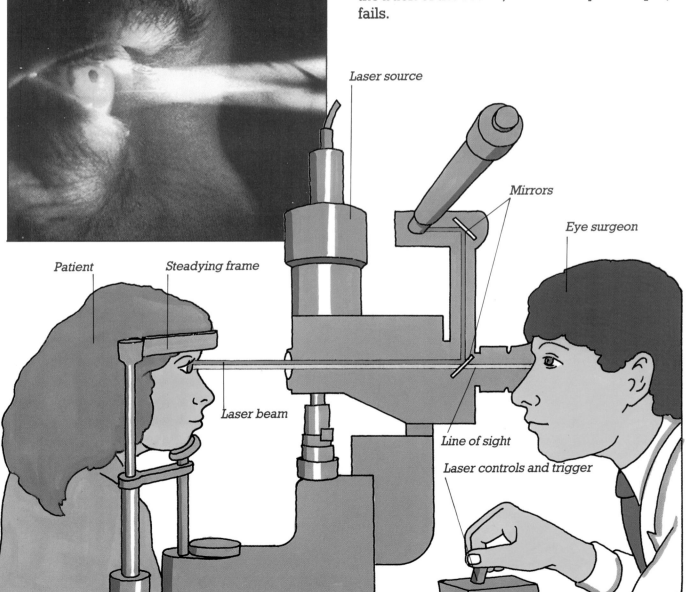

Laser source

Mirrors

Eye surgeon

Patient

Steadying frame

Laser beam

Line of sight

Laser controls and trigger

A detached retina

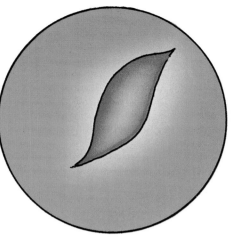

Torn area becomes detached

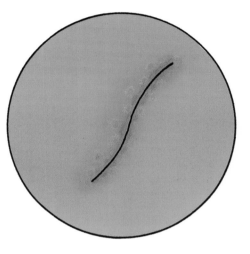

Retina re-sealed onto choroid

Reattached retina

A retina that has become torn or detached can often be treated by laser surgery. Tiny burns that reattach the retina to the choroid are made, starting round the edges of the detachment, where separation is least, and progressing to the middle. The surgeon pushes the wall of the eyeball in toward the retina, to narrow the gap, and fires the laser repeatedly to seal it against the choroid. The retina gradually floats back down as pockets of fluid under it are absorbed. Weak-looking areas in the other eye may be treated at the same time.

Retina after surgery

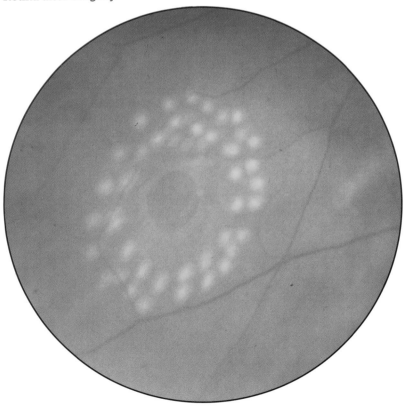

Before and after surgery

Through the ophthalmoscope, a detached retina can be seen (top). After laser surgery, the retina is fixed back onto the choroid by many tiny burns, like "spot welds," which show up as yellow dots (above). Provided the burns are not near the back of the retina, vision is largely unaffected.

LIVING WITH BLINDNESS

Although "blindness" is a common term, few people are totally blind and unable even to tell the difference between light and dark. Much more common is "visual impairment" or "visual handicap," in which sight is blurred, dimmed, restricted in visual field, or impaired in some other way. A rough definition of visual impairment is being unable to see clearly enough to count fingers at a distance of ten feet in ordinary daylight. Being visually handicapped does not necessarily mean being handicapped in other ways. One of the biggest problems facing such people is the attitude of someone who assumes that because they cannot see clearly, they cannot think clearly either. Because most of us rely on sight for so many daily activities, "blind" people are at a disadvantage unless provisions are made. This need not be expensive or inconvenient to others. It is more a question of good planning and understanding.

Guide dogs

For some visually handicapped people, a guide dog provides "eyes" and allows greater independence. Breeds with good intelligence and an even temperament are favored. For example, labradors, golden retrievers and German shepherd dogs. Usually a dog has up to six months of intensive training, which starts when it is about one year old.

"Seeing" with sound

"Ultrasonic eyeglasses" send out a beam of ultrasonic sound waves, too high in pitch for humans to hear. The waves bounce off objects, and their echoes are detected by a receiver, which turns them into sounds. A "mechanical dog" (far right) works in a similar way.

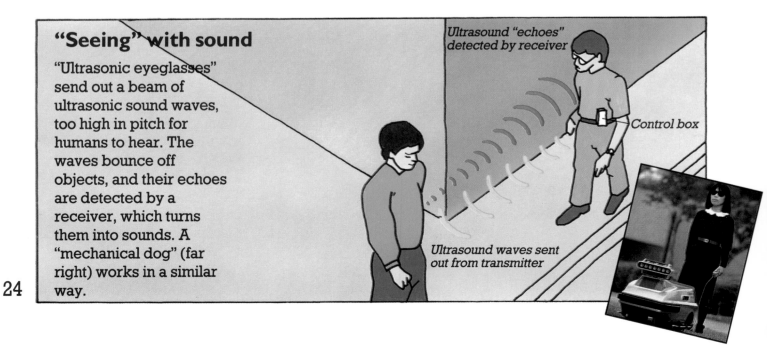

Ultrasound "echoes" detected by receiver

Control box

Ultrasound waves sent out from transmitter

Braille

The Braille system of touch-reading was invented in 1829 by Frenchman Louis Braille, blinded by an injury when three years old. Today there is a standard system for English-speaking peoples. Patterns of up to six raised dots represent letters, numbers and simple sounds and words. The dots are felt by the fingertips (right).

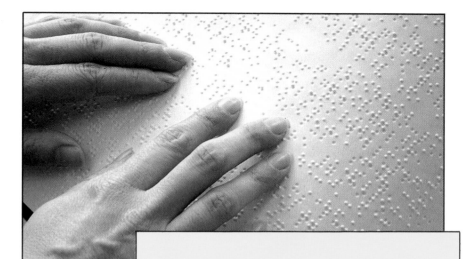

Reading machines

The blind student shown below is using a print-to-voice reading machine in a library. It converts printed material into synthetic speech. The machine can read clear type, but not handwriting, at a speed of up to 250 words per minute. It can be slowed down to spell out words. Blind people who have used this kind of machine find they can read text, without pictures or diagrams, easily. A beginner normally takes about an hour to learn to use the machine and more practice is needed to read pages with integrated pictures and text. Another device can translate print into Braille. The text is scanned with one hand and the other hand is used to feel the Braille display. Unfortunately, these machines are expensive and are mainly used in schools and libraries.

The Braille alphabet

25

Talking books

Only four percent of all blind people read Braille. In the United States, fewer than one in six visually handicapped children can use this system. For many who cannot see well enough to read, cassette tapes or "talking books" are particularly important. The tapes may be recordings of lessons, for schoolwork, or of speakers reading books which the listener can enjoy. Many well known actors and orators give their services for recording (below). Tapes can be borrowed from libraries, bought by individuals, or bought by schools and shared.

The computer revolution

Some blind people become expert at using computers for various jobs. A special keyboard with touch-patterned keys enables them to type in information accurately. Instead of a normal printer, they may use a Braille-embossing printer. Or a speech synthesizer may "speak" the results out loud. More complex systems turn normal printed matter into Braille automatically. An OCR (optical character reader) "scans" the printed page, detects the letters and numbers, codes them and feeds this information into the computer, which then prints out a Braille version on the embossing printer.

Improving appearance

Some people who have suffered eye injury or disfigurement may want to alter their appearance. By trying to look more "normal," they may feel they are helping to make others feel less nervous and awkward. There are various ways of achieving this, from the artifical "glass eye" (usually plastic) to a special cosmetic mask. Some visually handicapped people prefer to wear darkened glasses. This is an accepted sign, indicating that they cannot see properly. The most common sign is carrying a white stick. There are several types of stick. Short sticks mean the holder is visually impaired, while long sticks indicate total blindness.

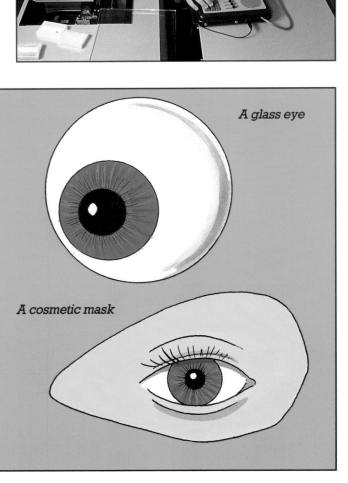

A glass eye

A cosmetic mask

EVERYDAY LIFE

Blindness or a degree of visual handicap affects different people in different ways. Those who have been blind since birth may well learn how to cope and deal with everyday problems. In former times blind children were taught in separate, special schools. Nowadays about half of visually handicapped children attend ordinary schools wherever possible, so that they feel part of normal society. This also helps other children to understand the difficulties posed by lack of sight. There are many modern aids and gadgets that allow visually handicapped people to do everyday tasks such as cooking, cleaning, shopping and gardening. Recently, raised images (below left) have been produced and displayed in art galleries to help visually-impaired people understand tape-recorded descriptions and commentaries about the paintings. This helps people with poor sight to make the most of their remaining useful sight. Many are able to work in jobs where eyesight is not essential, such as telecommunications, computers or the music industry. Many sports and leisure activities are also possible (below).

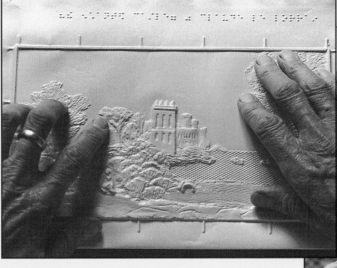

HELPING THE BLIND

There are times when partially sighted or blind people need help from sighted people. The sighted person may feel unsure of how to help. A blind person will probably appreciate being helped across the road. Do not be afraid to link arms with the person you are helping. For walking side-by-side indoors or out, stand by the person with your arms straight and fingers pointing to the ground. Ask your partner to take your arm. By holding your arm like this, the blind person will be half a pace behind you, making it easier to tell when you are turning, by your movements.

27

CARING FOR YOUR EYES

Eyesight is precious. Without it you could not read this book. So take care of your eyes and safeguard this most valuable of senses. Never poke or push things into your eyes. Do not look at the Sun or very bright lights. Visit the optician regularly, and always report any visual problems, pain or eye injuries to a doctor immediately. If you are prescribed eyedrops, make sure they are put in correctly and follow the instructions on the container. Be careful when playing – eyes could be at risk during incidents such as flicking objects into the face. "Accidents happen," and knowing you were responsible for somebody losing their sight can be a terrible burden of guilt.

The eyelids are there to protect your eyes from danger and the eyebrows help to trap tiny dust particles and keep dust out. Glands around the eye secrete liquid, that is distributed by blinking. Any irritating vapors or objects are washed away by an excess flow of unemotional tears.

Lighting

When you read or do close work, make sure you are in a good light. Do not strain your eye muscles – and your head and neck muscles – by screwing up your eyes and trying to see in poor light (above). You could suffer from sore eyes and headaches. Try to arrange for an even amount of illumination rather than one powerful source such as a spotlight. If you have only one light, it is better if it shines from the left if you are right-handed, so you are not writing in a shadowed area.

Ultraviolet rays

In recent years, sunbathing and tanning salons have become popular. It is wise to guard your eyes because certain kinds of ultraviolet rays (the ones that give you a suntan) can be harmful, possibly damaging the light-sensitive cells in your eyes. In bright sunlight, it is important to wear good sunglasses that have ultraviolet filters in the lenses. Also, follow the instructions in a tanning salon, or seek advice from a doctor, about eye-protecting goggles to use when sunbathing. It is important to wear the goggles in a salon, and do not overdo the tanning time.

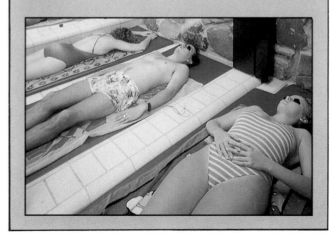

TV and computer screens

Watching a bright television in a dark room may lead to headaches and eye problems, because the eyes have trouble coping with the contrast of the bright picture in dark surroundings. Sitting too close to the screen may pose risks, perhaps from the electromagnetic radiation given off by the screen. Working for too long in front of a computer screen (visual display terminal) may also be harmful. Using a computer screen excessively can eventually damage your eyes. To be safe, you should only look at the screen for an hour at a time.

Eye protection

Machines such as cutters, grinders, sanders and welders can send tiny particles of wood, metal or plastic flying into the eye. This can happen at work, or doing tasks at home or in the garden. Operators should wear safety goggles or vizors to protect their face and eyes, and use the guards on the machines as instructed. People (especially children) who are watching should not put themselves at risk by coming too close. Chemicals such as weedkillers or paint-strippers may splash into the eye, with serious risk of scarring. Toys with sharp edges, can also be dangerous.

Care at play

The backyard or park is for having fun, but carefully. Do not throw sand or dirt around, or let other children do this – it could easily blow into someone's eyes. Beware also of animal droppings. These might contain eggs of a tiny worm named *Toxocara*. If the eggs get into the body, they may hatch and the worm can travel to the eye and lodge there, causing blindness. So wash your hands after playing outside. If *Toxocara* eggs infect a pregnant woman the newborn child may have inflammation of the choroid layer of the eye which may damage the retina and affect vision.

FIRST AID FOR THE EYES

In an accident involving the eyes, act at once. It is best to find a person trained in first aid. But if there is nobody skilled, follow the instructions given here and find medical advice as quickly as possible. Eye injuries should always be checked by a doctor.

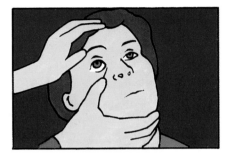

EXAMINING THE EYE
If someone feels pain or has a piece of dirt in the eye, hold the lids apart gently and look at the white and pupil of the eye in good light.

WASHING THE EYE
If something splashes into the eye, wash it out quickly with cool, running water. Try not to wash or spill water into the other eye.

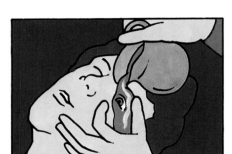

BATHING THE EYE
Use lukewarm water with a little salt added to bathe and soothe sore eyes, for example after exposure to smoke. Eyedrops can help too.

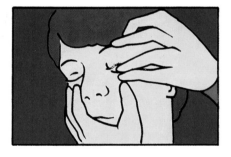

REMOVING AN EYELASH
If an eyelash has fallen into your eye, it may help if you pull the top eyelid over the lower one.

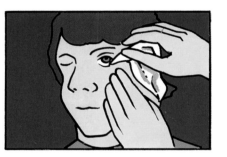

REMOVING A FOREIGN BODY
Lift off a speck of dirt or small fly with the moistened corner of a handkerchief.

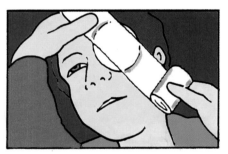

DRESSING THE EYE
Place a clean pad gently on the eye and bandage in place. To avoid further pain, so not use much pressure.

Useful information

The American Foundation for the Blind (AFB)
15 West 16th Street
New York NY 10011
A national nonprofit organization to improve the standards of service for blind and visually impaired people. The AFB provides direct assistance and referral services. Its headquarters are in New York City with regional centers in Atlanta, Chicago, Dallas, San Francisco and Washington DC.

Blind Outdoor Leisure Development
533 East Main Street
Aspen CO.81611
tel: (303) 925-8922
Forms local clubs for blind people engaging in outdoor sports, trains leaders and encourages reduced rates for local sports activities.

Asscociation of Radio Reading Services
PO Box 847, Lawrence, KS 66044
Tel: (913) 864-4600
Promotes radio reading services.

GLOSSARY

Astigmatism This is caused by the curve of the lens and cornea in the eye not matching. To correct the problem, glasses with a cylindrical lens are prescribed.

Blind spot The small area at the back of the retina where nerve fibers meet and leave the eye to become the optic nerve. There are no rods and cones at the blind spot and so it is insensitive to light.

Braille A system of printing and writing for the blind in which letters of the alphabet are made by raised dots that people can distinguish using their fingers. The system was invented by the Frenchman, Louis Braille in 1829.

Cataract The lens in the eye becomes opaque rather than transparent which causes problems in seeing. In older people it is often caused by a hardening of the lens. The treatment involves removal of the lens and patients have to wear glasses after the operation because they have no lens of their own.

Color blindness This is more correctly called "color-defective vision." It is an inability to distinguish colors. The most common defect is an inability to distinguish between red and green. Men are affected about three times more frequently than women.

Cone One of the light-sensitive receptor cells in the retina of the eye, responsible for distinguishing colors.

Conjunctivitis An inflammation of the thin transparent membrane, the conjunctiva, covering the front of the eye.

Contact lens A lens worn on the eyeball so that it is almost invisible. They are used by people who do not like to or cannot wear glasses. They are useful during sporting activities.

Glaucoma A disease caused by an increase of fluids in the eyeball, raising the pressure inside the eyeball.

Macula A small yelloe area in the inner surface of the retina at the back of the eye.

Ophthalmoscope An instrument used for looking at the back of the interior of the eyeball. It has a system of lenses through which the examiner looks along the path of a beam of light projected from the instrument.

Optic nerve The nerve along which sensory signals travel from the retina of the eye to the brain.

Retina Inner layer of the eyeball, formed by the expansion of the optic nerve which contains the rods and cones and receives visual rays of light.

Retinitis pigmentosa A disease that causes inflammation or white spots on the retina that can eventually lead to blindness.

Rhodopsin The light-sensitive pigment, sometimes called visual purple, found in the rod cells of the retina.

Rod One of the kinds of sensitive nerve endings in the retina of the eye. Rods do not distinguish between colors but do respond to dim light and so provide colorless night vision.

Stereoscopic vision This is when each separate eye "sees" two slightly different views of the same scene side by side.

Trachoma An eye disease that affects the cornea and the conjunctiva that can eventually lead to blindness. It is widespread in tropical countries, because it is spread by flies.

Visual field The area which can be seen without moving the eyes.

INDEX

CREDITS:
With special thanks to Angela Kirby and the pupils of
Harriet Costello School, Hampshire, UK.

Photographic Credits:
Cover and pages 18: Frank Spooner Agency; pages 5 both, 6t,
10 and 14: Biophoto Associates; pages 6b, 9t, 13 both, 16, 17t
and 28t: Roger Vlitos; pages 9b, 12t, 17b, 24b, 25 both, 26r, 29tl
and 29tr: Science Photo Library; pages 12b,
24t and 27tr: Magnum Photos; pagese 15, 19 and 23 both:
National Medical Slide Bank; pages 22 and 27b: Topham Photo
Library; pages 26l and 29b: Zefa; page 27tl: Steve Coward;
page 28b: Barry Lewis/Network.

PRINTED IN BELGIUM BY
proost
INTERNATIONAL BOOK PRODUCTION